Hyperquilting!

*Embellishing Your Free Motion Quilting
Designs with Decorative Threads*

by **Patsy Thompson**

Hyperquilting!
Embellishing Your Free Motion Quilting
Designs with Decorative Threads
Written by Patsy Thompson
Design and Illustration by Debra Davis Rezeli

2009 Published by Patsy Thompson Designs. All rights reserved.
Copyright © 2009 by Patsy Thompson & Ernie Bode

Patsy Thompson
[www.patsythompsondesigns.com]

ISBN 0615345948
EAN-13 9780615345949
Library of Congress Control Number 2010900002

SECOND PRINTING

Printed in Hong Kong

1

Introduction

2

Simple Flower-Based Designs

3

Complex Flowers Hyperquilting Designs

4

Hyperquilting Vines And Leaves

5

Epilogue

1

Introduction

Figure 1

Hyperquilting is my name for a 2-step technique where a "baseline" quilting design is first stitched in one thread, and then a secondary design is hyperquilted, or over quilted, right on top of it! This technique may be used to create background quilting designs, (see figure 1), and it may also be used to add intricacy to "stand-alone" quilted motifs such as feathers or vines and leaves. (See figures 2 and 3). Most of all, though, it is a fun and exciting way to add drama, excitement, and more detail to a quilt. On top of that, it is a wonderful way to add more texture and color through the judicious use of thread.

This book will be your guide to learning how to create a variety of eye-catching hyperquilting designs. Before we begin the designs, though, there are a few general guidelines to help you make the most of your hyperquilted embellishment. Some of these guidelines will have little meaning to you until after you've stitched out some of these designs on your own, so come back and re-read this section once you've got some experience under your belt.

Figure 2

- Thread choices matter. You are going to an awful lot of trouble to add this secondary design, so you want to make sure it will be seen! This means choosing a thread color that has good contrast with the background fabric and good contrast with the thread used to quilt the baseline quilting design.

- Avoid variegated threads for hyperquilting. (See figure 4). Although they are eye-catching and beautiful threads, the repeated color changes will be distracting in this application.

- Solid color rayon threads and trilobal polyester threads are ideal for hyperquilting. (See figure 5). They each have a sheen and luster that will attract the viewer's attention, but in an understated way. Metallic threads can also

Figure 3

add high drama, but be cautious here as some metallic threads are quite fragile and shred easily. Because hyperquilting frequently involves overstitching your designs multiple times, this is not a place for "sissy threads," and let's face it, those metallic threads are sissies!

- Use your time wisely. Hyperquilting will take extra time, so do not waste your efforts by stitching these designs on a busy background fabric where they will compete for attention and most probably be lost. (See figure 6). Remember, you are going to extra trouble to create this embellishment, so you want to be sure it will be seen!

Introduction \ Chapter 1

Figure 4

As you practice these designs, it is my hope that you will begin to realize that many, many designs have the potential to be enriched by hyperquilting. Sometimes, a baseline design may need to be slightly altered in order to accommodate a secondary design and other times, it will not need any alteration. Either way, if you can expand your thinking and allow yourself the freedom to play with design ideas, you will begin coming up with all kinds of intriguing designs on your own. I am merely introducing you to a concept; it is up to you to take that leap! Get your machine set up in free motion, straight stitch mode and get ready to have some fun. Now, let's get to the designs!

- Size matters! (No, I'm not talking about that!) Many hyperquilting designs involve stitching a secondary design inside of the primary or baseline quilting design. If the primary design is not large enough to support that secondary design, then the result will be an overcrowded mess. Always take the time to inspect your baseline design to ensure it really is large enough to accommodate hyperquilting and remember, the natural enemy of hyperquilting is overcrowding!

- Remember that the goal of hyperquilting is to enhance the underlying quilted design. This means that each hyperquilted design should respect the curves of the underlying baseline design, and you'll want to pay close attention to size and proportion as you work. Be prepared to modify each hyperquilting design to accommodate and enhance that baseline design as the one outcome you never want in hyperquilting is to create a sense of overcrowding.

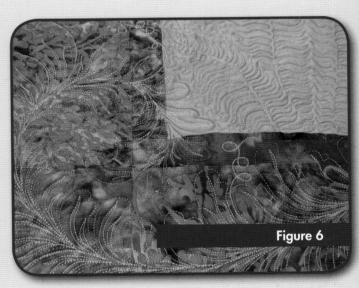
Figure 6

A Tip on How to Use the Diagrams and Instructions that Follow:

For each free motion quilting design, there will be stepwise instructions accompanied by an illustration. Each written step is numbered and color coordinated with the corresponding stitching step in the illustration.

For example, STEP 1 in the text is labeled blue, and that corresponds with the blue stitching line in the illustration above it.

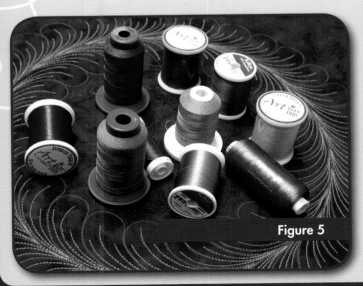
Figure 5

2

Simple Flower-Based Designs

Figure 7

The Loop-D-Loop Basic Flower

One thing you will learn as you delve into hyper-quilting is that all hyperquilting designs begin with a baseline design. Each of the hyperquilting designs in this chapter begins with the same baseline design, the loop-d-loop basic flower. (see figure 7). This design begins as a simple loop-d-loop background fill design, and the flower is randomly inserted between loops. The flower is a continuous line design that is created by rotating a series of petals around a central axis point. Here are the steps to creating the loop-d-loop basic flower design:

STEP 1: With your sewing machine set up in free motion, straight stitch mode, create a short expanse of the loop-d-loop design by crossing lines to create a loop, then stitch a nice curvaceous "travel line" to get yourself to the next spot to form a loop. When you wish to add a flower, stitch a fairly straight "travel line" to get yourself to the center of what will become the flower.

TIP: *Avoid making your travel line curved, or it will be very difficult to add your petals without intersecting that travel line.*

STEP 2: Hugging the stitching line that you created to get to the center of the flower, reverse direction and stitch a mitten-shaped petal. This will again take your stitching line back to the center of the flower.

STEP 3: Continue adding mitten-shaped petals that rotate around that center point of the flower. You can avoid "open spaces" between the petals if you hug the stitching line of the preceding petal each time you exit the flower's center.

TIP: *By adding a slight curve to your petals, you can add a sense of gentle movement to your quilting design.*

STEP 4: Once your petals have been stitched, you may exit the flower between any 2 petals. Stitch a short run of the loop-d-loop travel design and when you have enough space to begin stitching a new flower, stitch a short straight line to the flower's center and begin adding petals as detailed before.

Figure 8

The Basic Flower With A Sunburst Center Hyperquilting Design

The basic flower with a sunburst center (see figure 8) has some drama and punch when compared to the baseline design. This is a quick and easy hyperquilting embellishment, so it is a good place to start if you are new to hyperquilting and want to get your feet wet. Because the hyperquilting involves repeatedly stitching back and forth to the center of the flower, it is also a good way to cover up mistakes if you had some difficulty bringing your petal stitching lines back to the flower's center! Know that you can create a very different looking flower merely by extending some of the splay lines further into the petal, so be sure to try this variation as well.

STEP 1: With your machine set up in free motion, straight stitch mode and using a high contrast decorative thread, begin stitching a short run of the loop-d-loop travel line right next to the original stitching line.

TIP: *Avoid stitching directly on top of the original stitching line. By stitching alongside it and periodically crossing it, you will create a flowing ribbon-like effect.*

STEP 2: Beginning at the flower's center, stitch a short, slightly curved splay line, and then return to the center with your stitching line.

STEP 3: Stitch a second slightly curved splay line inside that same petal, but carry the stitching line a bit further into the petal, then return to the flower center again.

STEP 4: Repeat these same actions in each of the petals as you work your way around the flower. Always be aware of the size of the petal you are working in and adjust the number of sunrays to fill the size of that particular petal. (i.e. there may be room for only 1 or up to 3 sunrays in a given petal).

STEP 5: As you exit the flower's center to begin a new line of loop-d-loop, initially stitch directly on top of the previous loop-d-loop line, simply because there is not enough space for 2 stitching lines. Once your stitching line is again away from the flower petals, stitch just next to the previously stitched loop-d-loop stitching line, and deliberately cross it periodically to create a ribbon-like effect. When you enter the next flower, repeat the same process as above to create hyperquilted sunburst rays.

Figure 9

The Inlined Basic Flower Hyperquilting Embellishment

If you compare the inlined flower design (see figure 9) to the baseline flower design, you can really appreciate how much detail and interest inlining has added to this flower. Know that you can add complexity and interest to almost any shape through inlining, and the key to effective inlining is to always respect the underlying curves and shape of whatever structure you are inlining.

STEP 1: With your machine set up in free motion, straight stitch mode and using a high contrast decorative thread, begin stitching a short run of the loop-d-loop travel line right next to the original stitching line.

TIP: *Avoid stitching directly on top of the original stitching line. By stitching alongside it and periodically crossing it, you will create a flowing ribbon-like effect.*

STEP 2: Leave the flower's center and stitch a small version of the petal inside the first petal. This will bring the stitching line back to the flower's center.

STEP 3: Stitch a small, inlined petal inside each petal of the flower. As you work, be certain to alter your inlined petals so they are appropriate to the size of each petal you work within.

STEP 4: As you exit the flower's center to begin a new line of loop-d-loop, initially stitch directly on top of the previous loop-d-loop line, simply because there is not enough space for 2 stitching lines. Once your stitching line is again away from the flower petals, stitch just next to the previously stitched loop-d-loop stitching line, and deliberately cross it periodically to create a ribbon-like effect. When you enter the next flower, repeat the same process as above to create the inlining embellishment.

Figure 10

The Swirled Basic Flower Hyperquilting Embellishment

The swirled basic flower hyperquilting embellishment (see figure 10) is by far the most detailed design we have touched on thus far. In addition to adding a tremendous amount of complexity to the flower, it also adds just a hit of a sense of movement because of all the curving, swirling lines within the petals. The key to making this design look good is to slow down the stitching so that you can stitch right back over a swirl once you have stitched it. Any extraneous stitching outside the swirls will look messy and crowded, so take your time when stitching this design!

STEP 1: With your machine set up in free motion, straight stitch mode and using a high contrast decorative thread, begin stitching a short run of the loop-d-loop travel line right next to the original stitching line.

TIP: *Avoid stitching directly on top of the original stitching line. By stitching alongside it and periodically crossing it, you will create a flowing ribbon-like effect.*

STEP 2: Keeping fairly close to the lesser curvature of the petal, stitch a short swirl or curly-cue that curves inward, toward the middle of the petal, as opposed to curving toward the outer edge of the petal. Once you've reached the center of the swirl, reverse direction and stitch right over your already-stitched swirl line. This will carry the stitching line back to the center.

STEP 3: Stitch partway back up the first swirl stitching line, then curve outward and upward to stitch a second, larger swirl that moves into the tip of the petal. Once you've reached the center of the swirl, reverse direction and carry the stitching line back to the center of the flower.

STEP 4: Repeat this process inside each petal as you work your way around the flower. Notice that some petals are large enough to hold 3 swirls. When space allows, add a third swirl as you stitch your way back to the center from stitching the large second swirl.

TIP: *Be very careful about adding that third swirl and only do this when there is sufficient space. Remember: the natural enemy of hyperquilting is overcrowding, and it's very easy to go too far!*

STEP 5: As you exit the flower's center to begin a new line of loop-d-loop, initially stitch directly on top of the previous loop-d-loop line, simply because there is not enough space for 2 stitching lines. Once your stitching line is again away from the flower petals, stitch just next to the previously stitched loop-d-loop stitching line, and deliberately cross it periodically to create a ribbon-like effect. When you enter the next flower, repeat the same process as above to create the swirled embellishment.

3

Complex Flowers Hyperquilting Designs

Figure 11

The Basic Daisy

The designs in this chapter are all flowers with a center but the flower can be easily altered by changing the shape of the petals. Our first set of designs begins with the basic daisy (see figure 11) as the baseline design, and it is easily created as detailed below.

STEP 1: With your sewing machine set up in free motion, straight stitch mode, create a short expanse of the loop-d-loop design by crossing lines to create a loop, then stitch a nice curvaceous "travel line" to get yourself to the next spot to form a loop. When you wish to add a flower, stitch a fairly straight "travel line" to get yourself to the center of what will become the flower.

TIP: *Avoid making your travel line curved, or it will be very difficult to add your petals without intersecting that travel line.*

STEP 2: Stitch an oval or circle that will be the center of your flower.

TIP: *Notice that the circle or oval that is the flower center must be roughly perpendicular to the travel line that entered the flower. If it is not perpendicular, it will be impossible to stitch the petals coming off the flower center without intersecting the travel line that enters the flower.*

STEP 3: Hugging the stitching line that you created to get to the center of the flower, reverse direction and stitch a mitten-shaped petal. This will again take your stitching line back to the center of the flower.

STEP 4: Continue adding mitten-shaped petals that rotate around that center point of the flower. You can avoid "open spaces" between the petals if you hug the stitching line of the preceding petal each time you exit the flower's center.

TIP: *By adding a slight curve to your petals, you can add a sense of gentle movement to your quilting design.*

STEP 5: Once your petals have been stitched, you may exit the flower. Notice that you must exit between the first and last petals stitched. Stitch a short run of the loop-d-loop travel design and when you have enough space to begin stitching a new flower, stitch a short straight line to the flower's center and begin stitching your next basic daisy.

Figure 12

The Inlined Daisy Hyperquilting Embellishment

The inlined daisy hyperquilting embellishment (see figure 12) is very similar to the inlined basic flower, but adding that flower center adds a new level of sophistication to the design. If you've learned to stitch the earlier version, this should be easy for you to stitch.

STEP 1: With your machine set up in free motion, straight stitch mode and using a high contrast decorative thread, begin stitching a short run of the loop-d-loop travel line right next to the original stitching line.

TIP: *Avoid stitching directly on top of the original stitching line. By stitching alongside it and periodically crossing it, you will create a flowing ribbon-like effect.*

STEP 2: Leave the flower's center and stitch a small version of the petal inside the first petal. This will bring the stitching line back to the flower's center.

STEP 3: Stitch a small, inlined petal inside each petal of the flower. As you work, be certain to alter your inlined petals so they are appropriate to the size of each petal you work within.

STEP 4: As you exit the flower's center to begin a new line of loop-d-loop, initially stitch directly on top of the previous loop-d-loop line, simply because there is not enough space for 2 stitching lines. Once your stitching line is again away from the flower petals, stitch just next to the previously stitched loop-d-loop stitching line, and deliberately cross it periodically to create a ribbon-like effect. When you enter the next flower, repeat the same process as above to create the inlining embellishment.

Figure 13

The Daisy With A Sunburst Center Hyperquilting Embellishment

Although this design is fairly similar to the basic flower with a splayed center, the daisy with a sunburst center hyperquilting embellishment (see figure 13) is far more interesting and far more detailed. Know that this design can be dramatically altered merely by changing how far the sunburst rays delve into the flower petals, so it is well worth your time to try stitching this out in more than one way!

STEP 1: With your machine set up in free motion, straight stitch mode and using a high contrast decorative thread, begin stitching a short run of the loop-d-loop travel line right next to the original stitching line.

TIP: *Avoid stitching directly on top of the original stitching line. By stitching alongside it and periodically crossing it, you will create a flowing ribbon-like effect.*

STEP 2: Beginning at the flower's center, stitch a short, slightly curved splay line, and then return to the center with your stitching line. Stitch a second slightly curved splay line inside that same petal, but carry the stitching line a bit further into the petal, then return to the flower center again. Repeat as many times as you need to fill the first petal's base.

STEP 3: Repeat these same actions in each of the petals as you work your way around the flower. Always be aware of the size of the petal you are working in and adjust the number and lengths of sunburst rays to fill the size of that particular petal. (i.e. there may be room for more decorative stitching in one petal as opposed to another).

STEP 5: As you exit the flower's center to begin a new line of loop-d-loop, initially stitch directly on top of the previous loop-d-loop line, simply because there is not enough space for 2 stitching lines. Once your stitching line is again away from the flower petals, stitch just next to the previously stitched loop-d-loop stitching line, and deliberately cross it periodically to create a ribbon-like effect. When you enter the next flower, repeat the same process.

Figure 14

The Basic Dogwood Flower

The basic dogwood flower (see figure 14) is the baseline design for the next two hyperquilting designs. It is like a sister to the basic daisy and is created in much the same way, except that we have altered the petal shape. Know that you can create many other flower spin-off designs in much the same way, merely by making a small change in petal shape!

STEP 1: With your sewing machine set up in free motion, straight stitch mode, create a short expanse of the loop-d-loop design by crossing lines to create a loop, then stitch a nice curvaceous "travel line" to get yourself to the next spot to form a loop. When you wish to add a flower, stitch a fairly straight "travel line" to get yourself to the center of what will become the flower.

TIP: *Avoid making your travel line curved, or it will be very difficult to add your petals without intersecting that travel line.*

STEP 2: Stitch an oval or circle that will be the center of your flower.

TIP: *Notice that the circle or oval that is the flower center must be roughly perpendicular to the travel line that entered the flower. If it is not perpendicular, it will be impossible to stitch the petals coming off the flower center without intersecting the travel line that enters the flower.*

STEP 3: Hugging the stitching line that you created to get to the center of the flower, reverse direction and the first petal. This petal is shaped somewhat like a bird's beak. This will again take your stitching line back to the center of the flower.

STEP 4: Continue adding bird's beak-shaped petals that rotate around that center point of the flower. You can avoid "open spaces" between the petals if you hug the stitching line of the preceding petal each time you exit the flower's center.

STEP 5: Once your petals have been stitched, you may exit the flower. Notice that you must exit between the first and last petals stitched. Stitch a short run of the loop-d-loop travel design and when you have enough space to begin stitching a new flower, stitch a short straight line to the flower's center and begin stitching your next basic daisy.

Figure 15

The Inlined Dogwood Hyperquilting Embellishment

The inlined dogwood hyperquilted embellishment (see figure 15) is very similar to the inlined daisy hyperquilted embellishment. The only difference in stitching is that you will alter the shape of the inlining to echo the shape of the petal, so your inlined embellishment will also have a pointy tip.

STEP 1: With your machine set up in free motion, straight stitch mode and using a high contrast decorative thread, begin stitching a short run of the loop-d-loop travel line right next to the original stitching line.

TIP: *Avoid stitching directly on top of the original stitching line. By stitching alongside it and periodically crossing it, you will create a flowing ribbon-like effect.*

STEP 2: Leave the flower's center and stitch a small version of the petal inside the first petal. This will bring the stitching line back to the flower's center.

STEP 3: Stitch a small, inlined petal inside each petal of the flower. As you work, be certain to alter your inlined petals so they are appropriate to the size of each petal you work within.

STEP 4: As you exit the flower's center to begin a new line of loop-d-loop, initially stitch directly on top of the previous loop-d-loop line, simply because there is not enough space for 2 stitching lines. Once your stitching line is again away from the flower petals, stitch just next to the previously stitched loop-d-loop stitching line, and deliberately cross it periodically to create a ribbon-like effect. When you enter the next flower, repeat the same process as above

Figure 16

The Dogwood With A Sunburst Center Hyperquilting Embellishment

The sunburst center dogwood embellishment (see figure 16) is very similar to its daisy counterpart. In this case, the hyperquilting is identical, and only the petal shapes of the baseline designs differ.

STEP 1:   With your machine set up in free motion, straight stitch mode and using a high contrast decorative thread, begin stitching a short run of the loop-d-loop travel line right next to the original stitching line.

TIP: *Avoid stitching directly on top of the original stitching line. By stitching alongside it and periodically crossing it, you will create a flowing ribbon-like effect.*

STEP 2:   Beginning at the flower's center, stitch a short splay line, and then return to the center with your stitching line. Stitch a second splay line inside that same petal, but carry the stitching line a bit further into the petal, then return to the flower center again. Repeat as many times as you need to fill the first petal's base.

STEP 3:   Repeat these same actions in each of the petals as you work your way around the flower. Always be aware of the size of the petal you are working in and adjust the number and lengths of sunburst rays to fill the size of that particular petal. (i.e. there may be room for more decorative stitching in one petal as opposed to another).

STEP 5:   As you exit the flower's center to begin a new line of loop-d-loop, initially stitch directly on top of the previous loop-d-loop line, simply because there is not enough space for 2 stitching lines. Once your stitching line is again away from the flower petals, stitch just next to the previously stitched loop-d-loop stitching line, and deliberately cross it periodically to create a ribbon-like effect. When you enter the next flower, repeat the same process.

Figure 17

The Basic "Snowflake Flower"

In the next hyperquilting designs, the baseline design is the basic snowflake flower. See figure 17). This flower is really more of a "fantasy flower" in that it does not exist, but it also resembles a snowflake. Take care to stitch these snowflake flowers in a medium to large size; the petals are somewhat narrow in places so a small baseline motif would be very difficult to hyperquilt.

STEP 1: With your sewing machine set up in free motion, straight stitch mode, create a short expanse of the loop-d-loop design by crossing lines to create a loop, then stitch a nice curvaceous "travel line" to get yourself to the next spot to form a loop. When you wish to add a flower, stitch a fairly straight "travel line" to get yourself to the center of what will become the flower.

TIP: Avoid making your travel line curved, or it will be very difficult to add your petals without intersecting that travel line.

STEP 2: Stitch away from the center to create a petal shape that resembles an elongated shield; it should have 3 distinct points with the second point protruding out furthest from the center of the flower.

STEP 3: Continue adding petals all around the center of the snowflake flower.

TIP: *This design differs from the preceding flower designs in that you do not want to "hug" the preceding petal each time you begin to stitch a new petal. Your goal is to have some small spaces between each pair of petals.*

STEP 4: Once your petals have been stitched, you may exit the flower between any 2 petals. Stitch a short run of the loop-d-loop travel design and when you have enough space to begin stitching a new flower, stitch a short straight line to the flower's center and begin adding petals as detailed before.

Figure 18

The Snowflake Flower With A Sunburst Center

The snowflake flower with a sunburst center (see figure 18) should be reminiscent of the basic flower with the sunburst center. In addition to adding a nice colorful highlight to the center of the flower, this design is an easy way to cover up errors if you have not stitched a neat center to your baseline flower. Also know that an easy way to alter this design is to stitch your sunburst rays further into each petal. Again, small design alterations like this can create large changes in the perceived design.

STEP 1: With your machine set up in free motion, straight stitch mode and using a high contrast decorative thread, begin stitching a short run of the loop-d-loop travel line right next to the original stitching line.

TIP: *Avoid stitching directly on top of the original stitching line. By stitching alongside it and periodically crossing it, you will create a flowing ribbon-like effect.*

STEP 2: Beginning at the flower's center, stitch a short sunburst ray, and then return to the center with your stitching line.

STEP 3: Stitch a second sunburst ray line inside that same petal, but carry the stitching line a bit further into the petal, then return to the flower center again.

STEP 4: Repeat these same actions in each of the petals as you work your way around the flower. Always be aware of the size of the petal you are working in and adjust the number of sunrays to fill the size of that particular petal. (i.e. there may be room for only 1 or up to 3 sunrays in a given petal).

STEP 5: As you exit the flower's center to begin a new line of loop-d-loop, initially stitch directly on top of the previous loop-d-loop line, simply because there is not enough space for 2 stitching lines. Once your stitching line is again away from the flower petals, stitch just next to the previously stitched loop-d-loop stitching line, and deliberately cross it periodically to create a ribbon-like effect. When you enter the next flower, repeat the same process as above to create hyperquilted sunburst rays.

Figure 19

The Snowflake Flower With The Teardrop Hyperquilting Embellishment

The snowflake flower with the teardrop hyperquilting embellishment (see figure 19) is a much more complex appearing design, yet all we have done is to stitch an elongated teardrop inside of each flower petal. Because the central parts of each petal are fairly narrow, be sure to carry your teardrop shapes out fairly deeply toward the petal tip.

STEP 1: With your machine set up in free motion, straight stitch mode and using a high contrast decorative thread, begin stitching a short run of the loop-d-loop travel line right next to the original stitching line.

TIP: *Avoid stitching directly on top of the original stitching line. By stitching alongside it and periodically crossing it, you will create a flowing ribbon-like effect.*

STEP 2: Beginning at the flower's center, stitch an elongated teardrop shape inside the petal. This will return your stitching line back to the center of the snowflake flower.

STEP 3: Continue to stitch elongated teardrop shapes in each petal as you work your way around the center of the flower.

STEP 4: As you exit the flower's center to begin a new line of loop-d-loop, initially stitch directly on top of the previous loop-d-loop line, simply because there is not enough space for 2 stitching lines. Once your stitching line is again away from the flower petals, stitch just next to the previously stitched loop-d-loop stitching line, and deliberately cross it periodically to create a ribbon-like effect. When you enter the next flower, repeat the same process as above.

4

Hyperquilting Vines And Leaves

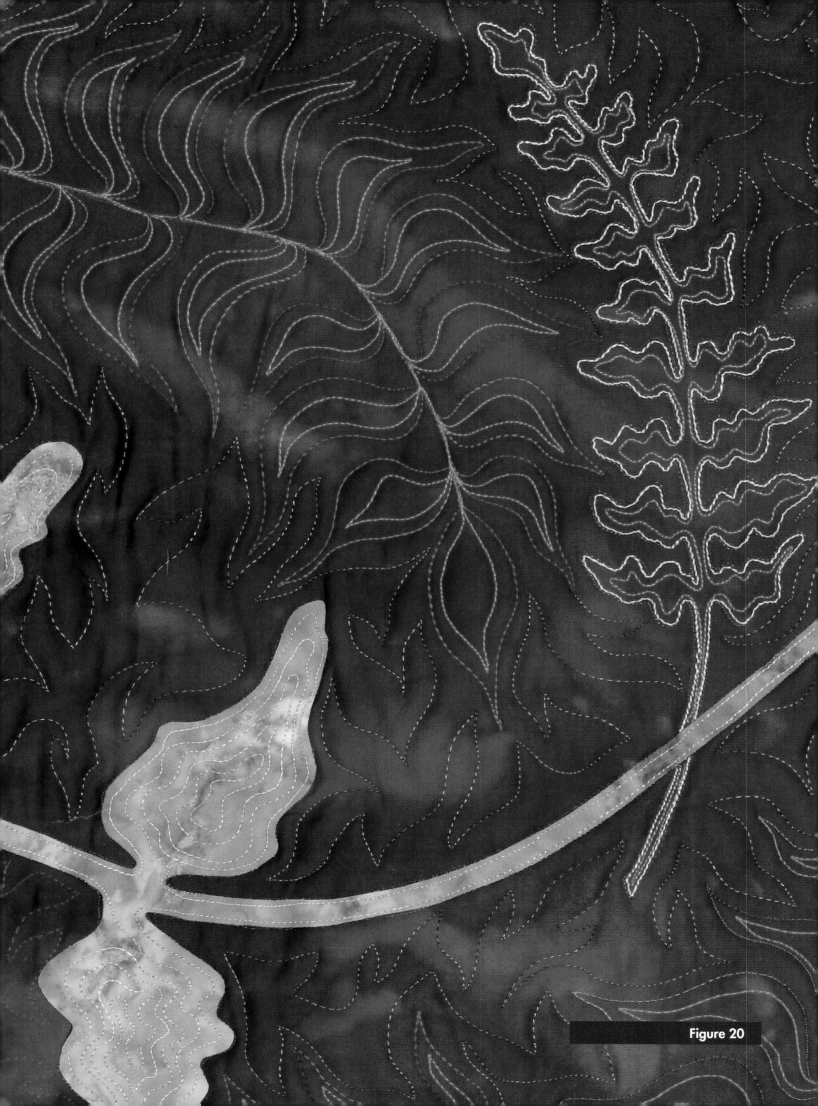

Figure 20

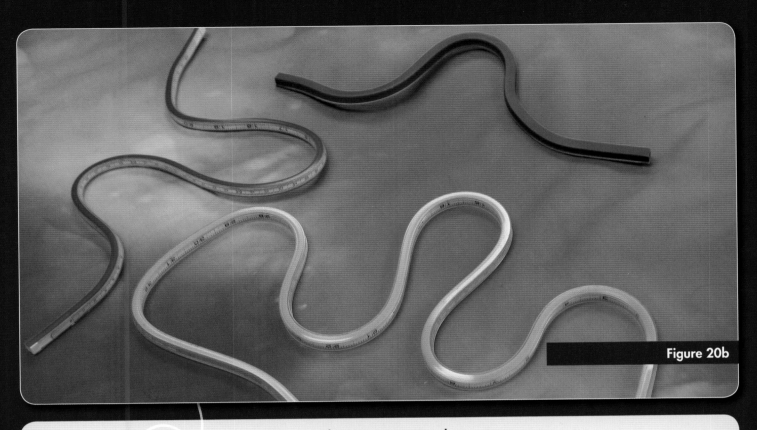

Hyperquilting Vines And Leaves

Vine and leaf motifs are wonderful substrates for hyperquilting. (See figure 20). Because of their meandering paths, vine and leaf motifs travel with seductive curves that capture the viewer's eye. Through hyperquilting, we can add detail and interest to vine and leaf motifs and this kind of "eye candy" is a reward to the viewer for taking a closer look.

To stitch any vine or leaf motif, you will need a flexible curve ruler. In figure 20b, there are flexible curve rulers of many sizes. The longer the ruler, the less time you will need to take in tracing your curves, so buy the longest ruler you can afford. You will also need some type of temporary marker, like a chalk marker, disappearing ink pen, soapstone marker, or a sliver of soap. It is always a good idea to test out a temporary marker on a scrap piece of fabric first to determine that it really will be temporary; ask me how I know this!

If you are planning to stitch the vine motif in a border area, you will bend your ruler within that border area so that it creates a pleasing curve that also leaves enough room for you to stitch out the vines and leaves. Once you have achieved a pleasing curve that fits your space, trace alongside the ruler with your temporary marker. To continue that curve beyond the length of the ruler, merely pick up the ruler, re-bend it to a curve that works for the adjacent space, and trace alongside it once again.

If you are planning to stitch vines in a non-border area (i.e. meandering between appliqué shapes), you will bend your ruler to create pleasing curves between these appliqué shapes and then trace alongside the ruler just as before. Take care not to stitch long vines (i.e. much more than about 12-18 inches in length) outside of border zones, or they can tend to visually "bisect" the design of the quilt top and this is generally not an intended result.

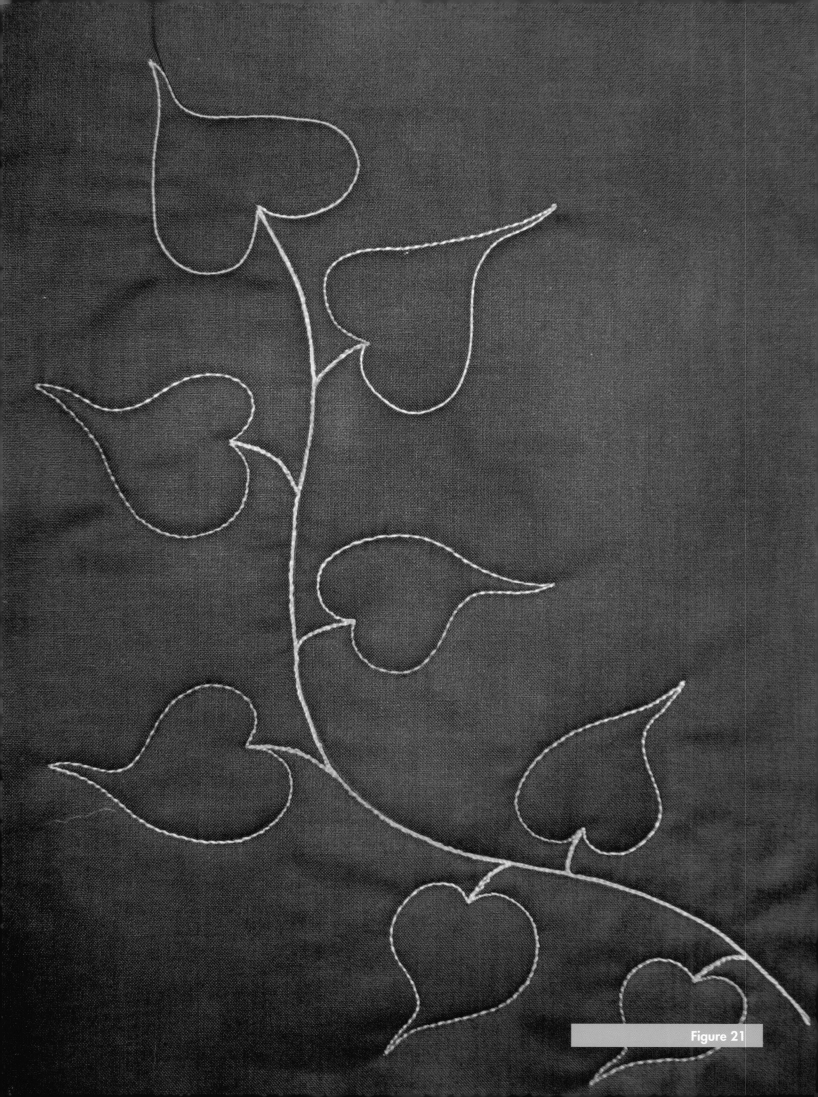

Figure 21

The Basic Curvaceous Vine

The basic curvaceous vine (see figure 21) appears somewhat ho-hum, boring, and vacuous. That's because it is! This vine must necessarily be a "bare-bones" design so that there is enough empty space for hyperquilting details to be filled in later on. This vine is easily stitched as below:

STEP 1: Once you have achieved a pleasing curve and created a stem guideline with a temporary marker, begin stitching from the base of the stem and stitch the entire stem line to where the very last leaf will be stitched.

STEP 2: Stitch the last leaf. In this case, the leaf is shaped like a potato vine leaf, which is a heart shape with a curvy tip.

TIP: *Know that this design can be stitched with a variety of different leaf shapes and it will take on different looks with each new shape.*

STEP 3: Stitch backwards, directly on the already stitched stem, until you reach a spot where you feel there is enough room to stitch the next leaf. Stitch a short stem to the leaf.

STEP 4: Stitch the next leaf.

TIP: *Know that as you proceed down the vine and add leaves, the leaves will be of many sizes, so do not feel a need to make them identical.*

STEP 5: Stitch backwards to get back to the main stem line and then continue the process of adding leaves when there is sufficient space. Periodically, leave a bit of additional room between leaves so there will be space to add grapevine curly-cues between some of the leaves.

Figure 22

The Hyperquilted Curvaceous Vine

You can see that the hyperquilted curvaceous vine (see figure 22) is far more interesting than its predecessor! Do not be intimidated by its perceived complexity; it is easily stitched, as detailed below.

STEP 1: Beginning with the needle at the base of the last leaf, enter the leaf and stitch the vein lines inside it.

STEP 2: Carefully stitch backwards, over the already stitched stem line, until you reach the short stem for the next leaf. Stitch up that short stem.

TIP: *Slow your stitching down as you stitch back over the already stitched stem or your work will appear messy.*

STEP 3: Enter the leaf and stitch the veins as before. Once done, stitch backwards down the short stem to the main stem, then to the next leaf where you will again add vein lines. Continue to repeat this process as you work your way down the vine.

STEP 4: When you reach a spot between 2 leaves where there is a bit more space, stitch a grapevine curly cue. This is really an intensely curled loop-d-loop, just like what we were stitching in earlier chapters. When you reach the end of the grapevine curly cue, reverse direction and stitch right back over the previously stitched line to arrive back at the main stem.

TIP: *Take care to stitch right over the already stitched curly cue. This will create a very heavy stitching line that will become a focal point of your design.*

STEP 5: Continue down the vine in this same way, adding vein lines in the leaves and grapevine curly cues where there is sufficient space.

Figure 23

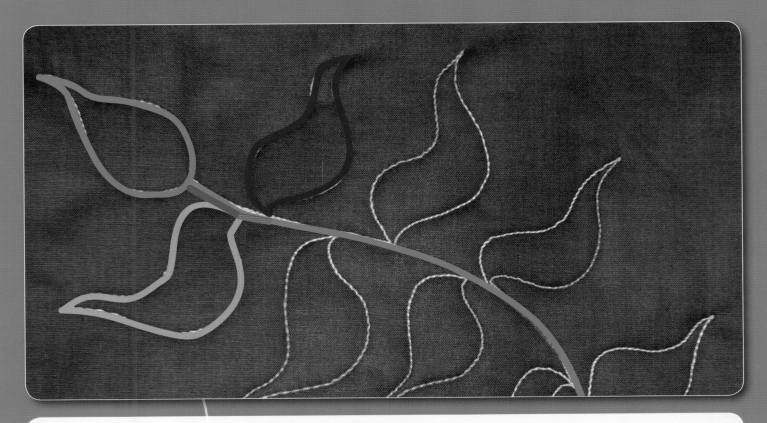

The Basic Aggressive Vine

The basic aggressive vine (see figure 23) is named so because it has the appearance of a somewhat menacing vine to me. I imagine that if one were asleep in the vicinity of this vine, one might awaken being strangled by it! Despite its menacing nature, it is an effective design for quilts and it is easily stitched, as detailed below.

STEP 1: Once you have achieved a pleasing curve and created a stem guideline with a temporary marker, begin stitching from the base of the stem and stitch the entire stem line to where the very last leaf will be stitched.

STEP 2: Stitch the very last leaf.

STEP 3: Stitch backwards over the already stitched stem until you arrive at a spot where there is sufficient space to stitch out the next leaf.

STEP 4: Stitch the next leaf.

TIP: *Notice that these leaves are not identical. There can be some variability is sizes and shapes of leaves and this can serve to make the design more interesting.*

STEP 5: Stitch backwards on the stem until there is space to stitch a leaf on the opposite side of them stem.

STEP 6: Stitch the next leaf, and then continue on in this way down the entire stem length.

TIP: *Be sure to leave sufficient space between the leaves of this vine for if they are stitched closely together, it takes on the appearance of a centipede!*

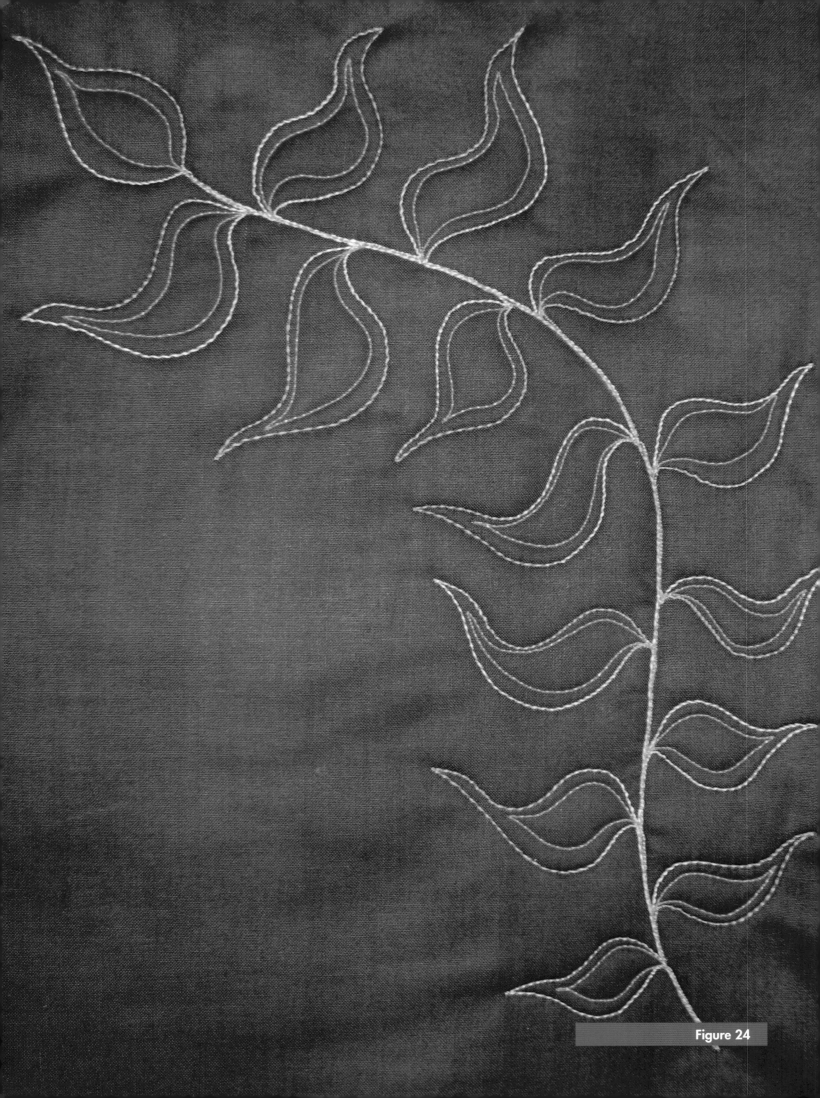

Figure 24

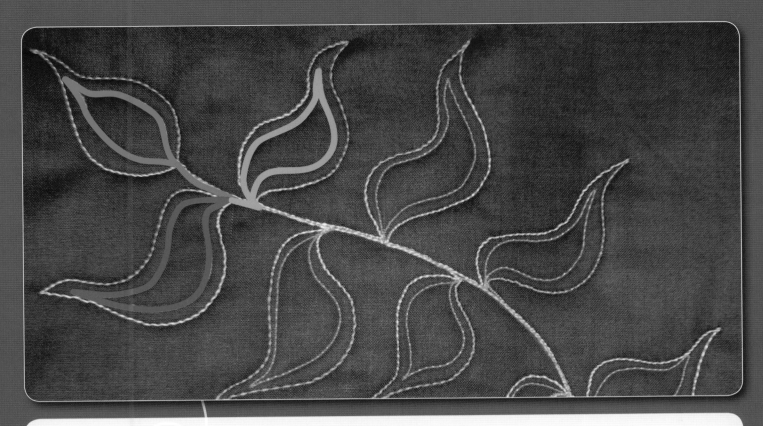

The Hyperquilted Aggressive Vine

The hyperquilted aggressive vine (see figure 24) has a far more complex appearance than its predecessor and this is simply by virtue of inlining each leaf. Know that almost any design can take on a look of complexity merely by inlining it.

STEP 1: Beginning with the machine needle at the base of the last leaf, enter the leaf and stitch a small leaf inside it.

STEP 2: Stitch backwards, directly over the already stitched stem line until you reach the base of the next leaf.

STEP 3: Enter the leaf and stitch a smaller, inlined leaf.

TIP: *Notice that each of the leaves you enter has a slightly different size and shape. As you inline, take care to echo the size and shape of each individual leaf in which you work.*

STEP 4: Stitch backwards on the stem line again until you reach the next leaf, then enter the leaf and inline each leaf as you work your way down the vine.

Figure 25

The Basic Whimsical Vine

The basic whimsical vine (see figure 25) has an element of fantasy to it. You can see that the addition of curly cues has made it a more fanciful and whimsical vine than the aggressive vine, so think of using it in your quilts where your goal is to add somewhat of a light-hearted and playful look. There is no rule about how many curly cues need to be added to the vine, so just stitch them out when you have sufficient space and the spirit moves you!

STEP 1: Once you have achieved a pleasing curve and created a stem guideline with a temporary marker, begin stitching from the base of the stem and stitch the very first leaf.

TIP: *Notice that this vine is different from the others in that the stem is not stitched ahead of time; you will create the stem as you work your way up it.*

STEP 2: Move to the opposite side of the stem guideline and stitch the first leaf on the opposite side.

STEP 3: Look at the stem guideline and the threads of the leaves that have been stitched. Stitch the next leaf on whichever side has more "blank space" between the stem guideline and the threads of the last leaf on each side. If you use this strategy as you work your way up the stem, you will be able to maintain the curve of the stem guideline. If there is an equal amount of space, then stitch the next leaf on whichever side you choose.

STEP 4: When you feel you have sufficient space, stitch a curly cue. Notice that these take up more space than the leaves, so be thoughtful about where you position them. Continue to work your way up the stem guideline, taking care to carry your stitching line all the way back to the last threads sewn.

TIP: *Your goal is to create a vine that has integrity; if the stitching lines are not consistently carried back to the threads of the last leaf or curly cue, the vine will look disjointed and not be believable.*

Figure 26

The Hyperquilted Whimsical Vine

The hyperquilted whimsical vine (see figure 26) should seem familiar to you. In it, we utilize the inlining technique. Just like with the aggressive vine, here we will inline each element with a smaller version of the "parent' element, and that will be either a leaf shape or a curly cue shape. Also like the aggressive vine, this simple hyperquilting technique adds a great deal of interest and complexity to the whimsical vine.

STEP 1:   Beginning with the machine needle at the base of the first leaf, enter the leaf and stitch a small leaf inside it.

STEP 2:   Enter the next leaf and stitch a small leaf inside it. Be sure to carry the stitching line all the way back to touch the threads of the last leaf. Continue up the stem in this manner until you reach the first curly cue.

TIP: *Notice that each of the leaves you enter has a slightly different size and shape. As you inline, take care to echo the size and shape of each individual leaf in which you work.*

STEP 3:   Enter the curly cue and stitch a smaller curly cue inside of it. When space becomes tight toward the tip of the curly cue, do not attempt to stitch further into the tip.

Remember, the natural enemy of hyperquilting is overcrowding!

5

Epilogue

Figure 27

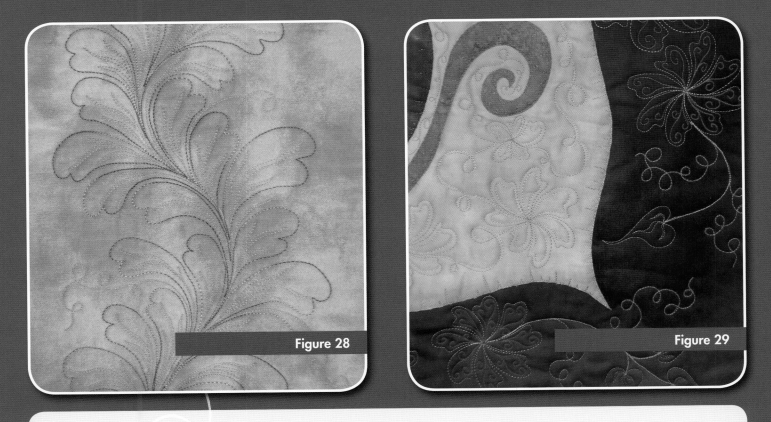

Figure 28

Figure 29

If you've been through the exercises to learn the designs in this book, then you have already taken the first steps to delve into the fun and exciting world of hyperquilting. When I introduce students to this technique in my free motion quilting classes, they are thrilled with the possibilities and they always wonder how I've come up with ideas like these. Truthfully, it's very easy as long as you are willing to expand your thinking beyond more traditional free motion quilting designs. What we've covered in this book is really only an introduction to the technique; kind of like a primer to help you get your feet wet. I'm hoping that you are now ready to dive into the pool!

As you challenge yourself to use hyperquilting in more complex designs (see Figure 27), you will find that it can completely transform the "personality" or ambience of the original quilted motif. Part of this transformation is due to the hyperquilted design itself and part of it is due to your thread choices. Always remember that you have the power to "amp up" the transformation through thread choices and you also have the power to make the transformation more subtle through thread choices. Decide what "ambience" you are trying to create through your quilting *before* you begin hyperquilting, and this will help guide you in making informed choices about which thread and which hyperquilting design can best help you achieve that end.

In your hyperquilting journeys, you will also discover that hyperquilting has the power to actually transform one quilted motif into an entirely different one. The hyperquilted heartleaf vine in Figure 28 actually began as a feather with modified plumes, but through hyperquilting, it has been transformed into a lovely meandering vine. Again, this is all through the judicious use of thread. This hyperquilting is powerful stuff!

If you take another look at Figure 28, you will notice that the grapevine curly cue from the hyperquilted basic curvaceous vine has been used in this design. If you can get into the habit of freely using design elements you have already learned and coupling them with other design elements (in this case, stylized vein lines), you will find that there is no limit to the design possibilities that are out there. This is again illustrated in Figure 29 where I have taken the basic flower with the swirled center and coupled it with the hyperquilted basic vine. Explore the infinite world of design possibilities by allowing yourself the freedom to pick and choose just how you would like to couple designs elements together. Trust me, this is a very fun and liberating adventure!

About the Author

Patsy Thompson was raised in an eastern suburb of Cleveland, Ohio and enjoyed many types of craftwork from an early age. She first learned to sew in a six-week sewing course at the local Singer store, and she's been hooked ever since! Initially a self-taught quilter in the late 1970's, Patsy's early ignorance of many of the rules of quilting led her down some new paths of discovery, learning all the joy and exhilaration that come with experimentation. Subsequent classes in numerous quilting techniques have fueled her fire and she now delights in the challenge of placing a new "spin" on different techniques.

Patsy was a hand quilter for her first 25-plus years in quilting and struggled to learn the art of free motion machine quilting. It wasn't easy! Once mastered, free motion machine quilting became a wonderful creative outlet and through teaching, Patsy now passes along her free motion mastery to others.

Patsy is best known in the quilting world for her series of instructional DVDs on free motion quilting that she co-produced with her husband, Ernie. Together, they have created eight different DVDs covering all types of free motion quilting designs and free motion techniques. Although Ernie is not a quilter, after spending countless hours behind a video camera and at a computer editing station, he thoroughly understands the process and enjoys adding his "spin" to each DVD. If you've ever met him at a quilt show, you know just how engaging his warm wit and sense of humor can be!

Ernie and Patsy divide their time between their homes in Holland, Ohio and Asheville, North Carolina. When they aren't busy creating quilting DVDs or books, they each work as practicing physicians.

NOTES

NOTES